Fraternal Charity

Fr. Benôit Valuy

2018

Originally published in 1908 by Benziger Bros.

Nihil Obtat
F. Thomas Bergh O.S.B.
Censor Deputatus

Imprimatur
+ Gulielmus
Episcopus Arindelensis,
Vicarius Generalis

Westmonasterii,
Die 7 Feb., 1908

© 2018 by Arouca Press
ISBN: 978-1-9994729-1-7

Arouca Press
PO Box 55003 Bridgeport PO
Waterloo, ON
Canada

Send inquiries to info@aroucapress.com

Cover art: *Christ Washing the Disciples' Feet*,
Giotto di Bondone (c. 1305)

Table of Contents

Translator's Note..vii

Introduction..viii

Charity the Peculiar Virtue of Christ.....................................1

First Fundamental Truth..2
    We are all members of the great Christian family.

Second Fundamental Truth..3
    We are members of the same religious family.

Family Spirit...5

Egotism, or Self-Seeking..7

First Characteristic...8
    To esteem our brethren interiorly

Second Characteristic...9
    To treat brethren with respect, openness, and cordiality

Third Characteristic..10
    To work harmoniously with those in the same employment, and not to cause any inconvenience to them

Fourth Characteristic..12
    To accommodate oneself to persons of different humour

Fifth Characteristic...14

To refuse no reasonable service, and to accept or refuse in an affable manner

Sixth Characteristic 15
To share the joys and griefs of our brethren

Seventh Characteristic 16
Not to be irritated when others wrong us

Eight Characteristic 18
To practise moderation and consideration

Ninth Characteristic 19
Care of the sick and infirm

Tenth Characteristic 20
Prayer for living and deceased brethren

Eleventh Characteristic 22
To have a lively interest in the whole Order, in its works, its success, and its failures

Twelfth Characteristic 23
Mutual Edification

Extent and Delicacy of God's Charity for Men 24

Extent and Delicacy of the Charity of Jesus Christ During His Mortal Life 25

First Preservative 27
How to fortify ourselves against uncharitable conversations, the principal danger to fraternal charity

Second Preservative 28

    To meditate on what the Saints say

Third Preservative...31
    To guard the tongue

Fourth Preservative...32
    To be on our guard with certain persons

Fifth Preservative...34
    To be cautious in letter-writing and visiting

Sixth Preservative...34
    Caution in communication with superiors

Seventh Preservative..36
    Caution in doubtful cases

Eight Preservative...37
    To check uncharitable conversation in others

Ninth Preservative..39
    How to check uncharitable conversation in superiors, etc.

Tenth Preservative..41
    Be cautious after hearing uncharitable conversation

Eleventh Preservative...42
    Not to judge or suspect rashly

Means to Support the Evil Thoughts and Tongues of Others..44

Second Means to Bear with Others.....................................46

Conclusion...47

Appendix 50
    The Practice of Fraternal Charity (Fr. Faber)
    Charitable Religious

Translator's Note

The name of Father Valuy, S.J., is already favourably known to English readers by several translations of his works, which have a large circulation.

The following little treatise is taken from one of his works on the Religious Life, and is translated with the kind permission of the publisher, M. Emmanuel Vitte, of Lyons.

The subject is so important a factor in community life that I feel confident it will supply a want hitherto felt by many. Though specially written for religious, it cannot fail to prove beneficial to seculars in every sphere of life, as love, the sunshine of existence, is wanted everywhere.

Introduction

The greatest commandment Our Lord gave is to love God and to love our neighbour. The two cannot be separated. St. John says in strong words that "if any man say, I love God, and hateth his brother; he is a liar. For he that loveth not his brother, whom he seeth, how can he love God, whom he seeth not?" (1 Jn. 4: 20). Charity then becomes the most fundamental virtue we as Catholics must foster.

Father Benoit Valuy, S.J., over a hundred years ago, wrote a short treatise on fraternal charity primarily for religious but applicable to every Catholic wishing to understand and live a life full of charity for one's neighbour.

Fraternal charity means that supernatural love we should have towards our neighbour who is either a child of God through grace or potentially so. As opposed to a vague humanism which treats man as supreme, fraternal charity does indeed love man but not for his own sake but for the sake of his eternal salvation – in God and through God. St. Thomas states:

> "Now the aspect under which our neighbour is to be loved, is God, since what we ought to love in our neighbour is to be loved, is God, since what we ought to love in our neighbour is that he may be in God. Hence it is clear that it is specifically the same act whereby we love God, and whereby we love our neighbour. Consequently the habit of charity extends not only to the love of God, but also to the love of our

neighbour."[1]

In the religious life, men and women, take vows of poverty, chastity, and obedience and live in common. The exercise of charity must become the cornerstone of this life otherwise it can become a cold, lifeless, and ineffectual means of perfecting souls especially consecrated to God. Personalities and temperaments will invariably clash but one of the aspects of the religious life should be the ability to overlook the faults of our brother exercising the type of charity that Our Lord displayed on earth and which He continues to exercise through His Church.

When we speak of charity at large the tendency is to equate it were mere "niceness" which presents a façade of congeniality but which has none of the toughness of spirit that real charity entails. Fr. Valuy is not speaking of this type of "charity"! To exercise fraternal charity requires a lively faith; it requires a supernatural vision capable of seeing the divine life in our confrere: "We need a pure gaze fitted to see the divine life of others under an envelope that at times is thick and opaque. We see the supernatural being of our neighbour if we merit to do so, if we are detached from self."[2]

Father Valuy's work gives religious practical means of achieving this detachment from their own wills in order to practice the type of charity Our Lord demands of

---

[1] *Summa Theologiae*, IIa-IIae, q. 25, a.1

[2] Fr. Reginald Garrigou-Lagrange, *The Three Ages of the Interior Life, Volume 2,* (Rockford, TAN, 1989), 207.

them. He strikes to the heart of that duplicity of spirit which can so easily put on the semblance of piety but which in reality is hypocritical in its dealings with other men. Fr. Valuy asks: "Am I one of those proud spirits who expose the faults of others in order to show off their pretended virtues?"

His work includes the writings of the Saints who show religious (and all of us) the necessity of charity towards all. As an example, in discussing the problems of uncharitable speech, St. John Climacus states: "For mercy's sake cease such conversation! How would you wish me to stone my brethren—me, whose faults are greater and more numerous?" We should treat others as we would want to be treated. It is such a basic principle yet how few take it to heart!

Religious who live each day with the faults of others, who perhaps transform the trifling annoyances of community life into mountains of tribulations, will see in this work a real program for developing a proper understanding of fraternal charity and the correct means of applying it.

We at Arouca Press have republished this small book with the hope that it will help inflame in souls a true charity for one's neighbour – that "bond of perfection" all are commanded to live. (Col. 3: 14)

Charity the Peculiar Virtue of Christ

Our Divine Saviour shows both by precept and example that His favourite virtue, His own and, in a certain sense, characteristic virtue, was charity. Whether He treated with His ignorant and rude Apostles, with the sick and poor, or with His enemies and sinners, He is always benign, condescending, merciful, affable, patient; in a word, His charity appeared in all its most amiable forms. Oh, how well these titles suit Him! a King full of clemency, a Lamb full of mildness. How justly could He say, "Learn of Me, that I am meek and humble of heart"! (Matt. 11: 29)

His yoke was sweet, His burden light, His conversation without sadness or bitterness. He lightened the burdens of those heavily laden; He consoled those in sorrow; He quenched not the dying spark nor broke the bruised reed.

He calls us His friends, His brothers, His little flock; and as the greatest sign of friendship is to die for those we love, He gave to each of us the right to say with St. Paul: "He loved me, and delivered Himself up for me" (Gal. 2: 20). Let us, then, say: "My good Master, I love Thee, and deliver myself up for Thee."

Religious, called to reproduce the three great virtues of Jesus Christ—poverty, chastity, and obedience—have still another to practise not less noble or distinctive—

viz., fraternal charity. By this virtue they are not called to rise above earthly or sensual pleasures, nor above their judgment and self-will, but above egotism and self-love, which shoot their roots deepest in the soul. They must consider attentively the fundamental truths on which charity is based and its effects, as also the principal obstacles to its attainment, and the means to overcome them.

First Fundamental Truth

We are all members of the great Christian family.

Charity towards our neighbour is charity towards God in our neighbour, because, faith assuring us that God is our Father, Jesus Christ our Head, the Holy Ghost our sanctifier, it follows that to love our neighbour—inasmuch as he is the well-beloved child of God, the member of Jesus Christ, and the sanctuary of the Holy Ghost—is to love in a special manner our heavenly Father, His only-begotten Son, together with the Holy Spirit. And because it is scarcely possible for religious to behold their brethren in this light without wishing them what the Most Holy Trinity so lovingly desires to bestow on them, acts of fraternal charity—include almost necessarily at least implicit acts of faith and hope; and the exercise of the noblest of the theological virtues thus often becomes an exercise of the other two.

Thus it is that charity poured into our hearts by the Holy Spirit, uniting Christians among themselves and with the adorable Trinity whose images they are, is the vivid and perfect imitation of the love of the Father for the Son, and of the Son for the Father—a substantial love which is no other than the Holy Ghost, and makes us all one in God by grace, as the Father and Son are only one God with the Holy Ghost by nature, according to the words of our Lord: "That they all may be one; as Thou, Father, in Me, and I in Thee: that they also may be one in Us." (Jn. 17: 21)

Such is the chain that unites and binds us—a chain of gold a thousand times stronger than those of flesh and blood, interest or friendship, because these permit the defects of body and the vices of the soul to be seen, whilst charity covers all, hides all, to offer exclusively to admiration and love the work of the hands of God, the price of the blood of Jesus Christ and the masterpiece of the Holy Spirit.

Second Fundamental Truth

We are members of the same religious family.

To love our brethren as ourselves in relation to God, it suffices without doubt to have with them the same faith, the same Sacraments, the same head, the same life, the same immortal hopes, etc. But, besides these, there exist other considerations which lead friendship and fraternity to a higher degree among the members of the same religious Order. All in the novitiate have been cast in the same mould, or, rather, have imbibed the milk of knowledge and piety from the breasts of the same mother. All follow the same rules; all tend to the same end by the same means; all from morning to night, and during their whole lives, perform the same exercises, live under the same roof, work, sanctify themselves, suffer and rejoice together. Like fellow-citizens, they have the same interests; like soldiers, the same combats; like children of a family, the same ancestors and heirlooms; and, like friends, a communication of ideas and interchange of sentiments.

If our Lord said to Christians in general, "This is My commandment, that you love one another as I have loved you. By this shall all men know that you are My disciples, if you have love one for another" (Jn. 13: 34), can He not say to the members of the same religious Order: "This is My own and special recommendation: Before all and above all preserve amongst you a mutual charity. Have but one soul in several different bodies. You will be recognized as religious and brethren, not by the same habit, vows, and virtues, nor by the particular work entrusted to you by the Church, but by the love you have one for the other. Ah who will love you if you do not love one another? Love one another fraternally, because as human beings you have only one heavenly Father. Love one another holily, because as Christians you have only one Head. Love one another tenderly, because as religious you have only one mother your Order"?

It is impossible for religious to love their brethren with a true, sincere, pure, and constant love if they do not look at them in this light.

Family Spirit

Based on the foregoing principles, fraternal charity begets the family spirit—that spirit which forgets itself in thinking only of the common good; which makes particular give way to general interests; which forces oneself to live with all without exception, to live as all without singularity, and to live for all without self-seeking; that spirit which, binding like a Divine cement all parts of the mysterious edifice of religion, uniting all hearts in one and all wills in one, permits the community to proceed firmly and securely, and its members to work out efficaciously and peacefully their personal sanctification and perfection; in fine, that spirit which gives to all religious not only an inexpressible family happiness, but a delicious foretaste of heaven, which renders them invincible to their enemies, and causes to be said of them with admiration: "See how they love one another!"

Writing on these words of the Psalmist, "Behold how good and pleasant it is for brethren to live together in union" (Ps. 132:1), St. Augustine cries out: "Behold the words which make monasteries spring up! Sweet, delightful, and delicious words which fill the soul and ear with jubilation."

Yes, certainly the happiness of community life is great and its advantages inappreciable; but without the family spirit there is no community, as there would be no beauty in the human body without harmony in its members. Oh, never forget this comparison, you who wish to live happy in religion, and who wish to make others happy.

A community is a body. Now, as the members of a body, each in its proper place and functions, live in perfect harmony, mutually comfort, defend, and love each other, without being jealous or vengeful, and have only in view the well-being of that body of which they are parts, so in the community of which you are members and in the employment assigned to you. Remember you are parts of a whole, and that it is necessary to refer to this whole your time, labour, and strength; to have the same thoughts, sentiments, designs, and language, without which there would no longer exist either body, members, parts, or whole. If you wish, then, to obtain and practise the family spirit, study what passes within you. Your actions bespeak your sentiments.

Egotism, or Self-Seeking

Egotism, taking for its motto "Every one for himself," is very much opposed to fraternal charity and the family spirit. It never hesitates, when occasion offers, to sacrifice the common good to its own. It isolates the individuals, makes them concentrated in self, places them in the community, but not of it, makes them strangers amongst their brethren, and tends to justify the words of an impious writer, who calls monasteries "reunions of persons who know not each other, who live without love, and die without being regretted."

Egotism breeds distrust, jealousy, parties, aversions. It destroys abnegation, humility, patience, and all other virtues. It introduces a universal disgust and discontent, makes religious lose their first fervour, presents an image of hell where one expected to find a heaven on earth, saps the very foundation of community life, and leads sooner or later to inevitable ruin.

As the family spirit causes the growth and prosperity of an order, however feeble its beginning, so, on the other hand, egotism dries the sap and renders it powerless, no matter what other advantages it may enjoy. If the one, by uniting hearts, is a principle of strength and duration, the other, by dividing, is a principle of dissolution and decay. Sallust says that "the weakest things become powerful by concord, and the greatest perish through discord." Whilst the descendants of Noah spoke the same language the building of the tower of Babel proceeded with rapidity. From the moment they ceased to understand one another its destruction commenced, and the monument which was to have immortalized their name was left in ruin to tell their shame and pride.

On each of the four corners of the monastery religion or charity personified ought to be placed, bearing on shields in large characters the following words: (1) "Love one another"; (2) "He who is not with Me is against Me, and he who gathers not with Me scatters"; (3) "Every kingdom divided will become desolate"; (4) "They had all but one heart and one soul."

First Characteristic

To esteem our brethren interiorly

"Charity, the sister of humility," says St. Paul, "is not puffed up." She cannot live with pride, the disease of a soul full of itself. It willingly prefers others by considering their good qualities and one's own defects, and shows this exteriorly when occasion offers by many sincere proofs. It always looks on others from the most favourable point. Instead of closing the eyes on fifty virtues to find out one fault, without any other profit than to satisfy a natural perverseness and to excuse one's own failings, it closes the eyes on fifty faults to open them on one virtue, with the double advantage of being edified and of blessing God, the Author of all good.

Since an unfavourable thought, or the sight of an action apparently reprehensible, tends to cloud the reputation of a religious, charity hastens before the cloud thickens to drive it away, saying, "What am I doing? Should I blacken in my mind the image of God, and seek deformities in the member of Jesus Christ? Besides, cannot my brethren be eminently holy and be subject to many faults, which God permits them to fall into in order to keep them humble, to teach them to help others, and to exercise their patience?"

Second Characteristic

To treat brethren with respect, openness, and cordiality

Exterior honour being the effect and sign of interior esteem, charity honours all those whom it esteems—superiors, equals, the young and the old. It carefully observes all propriety, and takes into consideration the different circumstances of age, employment, merit, character, birth, and education to make itself all to all. Convinced that God is not unworthy to have well-bred persons in His service, and that religious ought not to respect themselves less than people in the world, it conforms to all the requirements of politeness as far as religious simplicity will permit; not that politeness which is feigned and hypocritical, and which is merely a sham expression of deceitful respect, but that politeness, the flower of charity, which, manifesting exteriorly the sentiments of a sincere affection and a true devotion, is accompanied with a graceful countenance, benign and affable regards, sweetness in words, foresight, urbanity, and delicacy in business. In fine, that politeness which is the fruit of self-denial and humility no less than of charity and friendship; which is the art of self-restraint and self-conquest, without restraining others; which is the care of avoiding everything that might displease, and doing all that can please, in order to make others content with us and with themselves. In a word, a mixture of discretion and complaisance, cordiality and respect, together with words and manners full of mildness and benignity.

Third Characteristic

To work harmoniously with those in the same employment, and not to cause any inconvenience to them

Why should we cling so obstinately to our own way of seeing and doing? Do not many ways and means serve the same ends provided they be employed wisely and perseveringly? Some have succeeded by their methods, and I by mine—a proof that success is reached through many ways, and that it is not by disputing it is obtained, nor by giving scandal to those we should edify, nor, perhaps, by compromising the good work in which we are employed. The four animals mentioned by Ezekiel joined their wings, were moved by the same spirit and animated by the same ardour, and so drew the heavenly chariot with majesty and rapidity, giving us religious an example of perfect union of efforts and thoughts.

Charity avoids haughty and contemptuous looks, forewarns itself against fads and manias, and in the midst of most pressing occupations carefully guards against rudeness and impatience. Careful of wounding the susceptibility of others, it neither blames nor despises those who act in an opposite way. Religious animated by fraternal charity are not ticklish spirits who are disturbed for nothing at all, and who do not know how to pass unnoticed a little want of respect, etc.; nor punctilious spirits, who find pleasure in contradicting and making irritating remarks; nor self-opinionated spirits, who pose themselves as supreme judges of talent and virtue as well as infallible dispensers of praise and blame. Neither are they suspicious characters who are constantly ruminating in their hearts, and who consider every little insult as levelled at themselves; nor discontented beings, who find fault with the places whither obedience sends them and the persons with whom they live, and who could travel the entire world without finding a single place or a single person to suit them.

Charitable religious are not those imperious minds who endeavour to impose their opinions on all and refuse to accept those of others, however just they may be, simply because they did not emanate from themselves, nor are they those ridiculing, hard-to-be-pleased sort of people who do not spare even grey hairs. Finally, they are not those great spouters who, instead of accommodating themselves to circumstances as charity and politeness require, monopolize the conversation, and thereby shut up the mouths of others and make them feel weary when they should be joyful and free.

Fourth Characteristic

To accommodate oneself to persons of different humour

They who are animated by charity support patiently and in silence, in sentiments of humility and sweetness, as if they had neither eyes nor ears, the difficult, odd, and most inconstant humours of others, although they may find it very difficult at times to do so.

No matter how regular and perfect we may be, we have always need of compassion and indulgence for others. To be borne with, we must bear with others; to be loved, we must love; to be helped, we must help; to be joyful ourselves, we must make others so. Surrounded as we are by so many different minds, characters, and interests, how can we live in peace for a single day if we are not condescending, accommodating, yielding, self-denying, ready to renounce even a good project, and to take no notice of those faults and shortcomings which are beyond our power or duty to correct?

Charity patiently listens to a bore, answers a useless question, renders service even when the need is only imaginary, without ever betraying the least signs of annoyance. It never asks for exceptions or privileges for fear of exciting jealousy. It does not multiply nor prolong conversations which in any way annoy others. It fights antipathy and natural aversions so that they may never appear, and seeks even the company of those who might be the object of them. It does not assume the office of reprehending or warning through a motive of bitter zeal. It seeks to find in oneself the faults it notices in others, and perhaps greater ones, and tries to correct them. "If thou canst not make thyself such a one as thou wouldst, how canst thou expect to have another according to thy liking? We would willingly have others perfect, and yet we mend not our own defects. We would have others strictly corrected, but are not fond of being corrected ourselves. The large liberty of others displeases us, and yet we do not wish to be denied anything we ask for. We are willing that others be bound up by laws, and we suffer not ourselves to be restrained by any means. Thus it is evident how seldom we weigh our neighbour in the same balance with ourselves". (*Imitation*, Book 1:16)

Fifth Characteristic

To refuse no reasonable service, and to accept or refuse in an affable manner

Charity is generous; it does everything it can. When even it can do little, it wishes to be able to do more. It never lets slip an opportunity of comforting, helping, and taking the most painful part, after the example of its Divine Model, Who came to serve, not to be served. One religious, seemingly in pain, seeks comfort; another desires some book, instrument, etc.; a third bends under a burden; while a fourth is afflicted. In all these cases charity comes to the aid by consoling the one, procuring little gratifications for the other, and helping another. Without complaining of the increased labour or the carelessness of others, it finishes the work left undone by them, too happy to diminish their trouble, while augmenting its own reward. "Does the hunter," says St. John Chrysostom, "who finds splendid game blame those who beat the brushwood before him? Or does the traveller who finds a purse of gold on the road neglect to pick it up because others who preceded him took no notice of it?" It would be a strange thing to find religious uselessly giving themselves to ardent desires of works of charity abroad, such as nursing in a hospital or carrying the Gospel into uncivilized lands, and at the same time in their own house and among their own brethren showing coldness, indifference, and want of condescension.

There is an art of giving as well as of refusing. Several offend in giving because they do so with a bad grace; others in refusing do not offend because they know how to temper their refusal by sweetness of manner. Charity possesses this art in a high degree, and, besides, raises a mere worldly art into a virtue and fruit of the Holy Ghost.

Sixth Characteristic

To share the joys and griefs of our brethren

As the soul in the human body establishes all its members as sharers equally in joys and griefs, so charity in the religious community places everything in common content, affliction, material goods driving out of existence the words *mine* and *thine*. It lavishes kind words and consolations on all who suffer in any way through ill-humour, sickness, want of success, etc.; it rejoices when they are successful, honoured, and trusted, or endowed with gifts of nature or grace, felicitates them on their good fortune, and thanks God for them. If, on the one hand, compassion sweetens pains to the sufferer by sharing them, on the other hand participation in a friend's joys doubles them by making them personal to ourselves. Would to God that this touching and edifying charity replaced the low and rampant vice of jealousy!

When David returned after he slew the Philistines, the women came out of all the cities of Israel singing and dancing to meet King Saul. And the women sang as they played, "Saul slew his thousands and David his ten thousands." Saul was exceedingly angry, and this word was displeasing in his eyes, and he said: "They have given David ten thousand, and to me they have given but a thousand. . . . And Saul did not look on David with a good eye from that day forward. . . . And Saul held a spear in his hand and threw it, thinking to nail David to the wall" (1 Kings). Thus it is that the jealous complain of their brethren who are more successful, learned, or praised; thus it is that they lance darts of calumny, denunciation, and revenge.

Seventh Characteristic

Not to be irritated when others wrong us

We must pardon and do good for evil, as God has pardoned us and rendered good for evil in Jesus Christ. It is vain to trample the violet, as it never resists, and he who crushes it only becomes aware of the fact by the sweetness of its perfume. This is the image of charity. It always strives to throw its mantle over the evil doings of others, persuading itself that they were the effects of surprise, inadvertence, or at most very slight malice. If an explanation is necessary, it is the first to accuse itself. Never does it permit the keeping of a painful thought against any of the brethren, and does all in its power to hinder them from the same; and, moreover, excuses all signs of contempt, ingratitude, rudeness, peculiarities, etc.

Cassian makes mention of a religious who, having received a box on the ear from his abbot in presence of more than two hundred brethren, made no complaint, nor even changed colour. St. Gregory praises another religious, who, having been struck several times with a stool by his abbot, attributed it not to the passion of the abbot, but to his own fault. He adds that the humility and patience of the disciple was a lesson for the master. This charity will have no small weight in the balance of Him Who weighs merit so exactly.

Charity gives no occasion to others to suffer, but suffers all patiently, not once, but all through life, every day and almost every hour. It is most necessary for religious, as, not being able to seek comfort abroad, they are obliged to live in the same house, often in the same employment with characters less sympathetic than their own. These little acts of charity count for little here below, and they are rather exacted than admired. Hence there is less danger of vainglory, and all their merit is preserved in the sight of God.

Eight Characteristic

To practise moderation and consideration

Tell-tales, nasty names, cold answers, lies, mockery, harsh words, etc., are all contrary to charity. St. John Chrysostom says: "When anyone loads you with injuries, close your mouth, because if you open it you will only cause a tempest. When in a room between two open doors through which a violent wind rushes and throws things in disorder, if you close one door the violence of the wind is checked and order is restored. So it is when you are attacked by anyone with a bad tongue. Your mouth and his are open doors. Close yours, and the storm ceases. If, unfortunately, you open yours, the storm will become furious, and no one can tell what the damage may be." If we have been guilty in this respect, let us humble ourselves before God.

"The tongue," says St. Gertrude, "is privileged above the other members of the body, as on it reposes the sacred body and precious blood of Jesus Christ. Those, then, who receive the Holy of Holies without doing penance for the sins of the tongue are like those who would keep a heap of stones at their doors to stone a friend on arrival."

In order to keep ourselves and others in a state of moderation, we must remember that all persons have some fad, mania, or fixed ideas which they permit no one to gainsay. If we touch them on these points, it will be like playing an accompaniment to an instrument with one string out of tune.

Ninth Characteristic

Care of the sick and infirm

Charity lavishes care on the sick and infirm, on the old, on guests and new-comers. It requires that we visit those who are ill, to cheer and console them, to foresee their wants, and thereby to spare them the pain or humiliation of asking for anything.

Bossuet says: "Esteem the sick, love them, respect and honour them, as being consecrated by the unction of the Cross and marked with the character of a suffering Jesus."

Charity pays honour to the aged in every respect, coincides with their sentiments, consults them, forestalls their desires, and attempts not to reform in them what cannot be reformed. Charity receives fraternally all guests and new-comers, and makes us treat them as we would wish to be treated under similar circumstances. It also causes us to lavish testimonies of affection on those who are setting out, and warns us to be very careful of saying or doing anything that may in the least degree offend even the most susceptible.

Religious must ever feel that they can bless, love, and thank religion as a good mother. But religion is not an abstract matter; it is made up of individuals reciprocally bound together in and for each other.

Alas! how many times are the sick and the old made to consider themselves as an inconvenient burden, or like a useless piece of furniture! In reality what are they doing? They pray and do penance for the community, turn away the scourge of God, draw down His graces and blessings, merit, perhaps, the grace of perseverance for several whose vocation is shaking, hand down to the younger members the traditions and spirit of the institute, and finally practise, and cause to be practised, a thousand acts of virtue.

Did our Divine Lord work less efficaciously for the Church when He hung on the Cross than when He preached? We must, then, do for the sick and the old who are now bearing their cross what we would have wished to do for Jesus in His suffering.

Tenth Characteristic

Prayer for living and deceased brethren

"We do not remember often enough our dear dead, our departed brethren," says St. Francis de Sales, "and the proof of it is that we speak so little of them. We try to change the discourse as if it were hurtful. We let the dead bury their dead. Their memory perishes with us like the sound of the funeral knell, without thinking that a friendship which perishes with death is not true.

It is a sign of piety to speak of their virtues as it urges us to imitate them."

In communities distinguished for fraternal charity and the family spirit the conversation frequently turns on the dead. One talks of their virtues, another of their services, a third quotes some of their sayings, while a fourth adds some other edifying fact; and who is the religious that will not on such occasions breathe a silent prayer to God and apply some indulgence or other satisfactory work for the happy repose of their souls?

Charity also prays for those who want help most, and who are often known to God alone—those whose constancy is wavering, those who are led by violent temptations to the edge of the precipice. It expands pent-up souls by consolations or advice; it dissipates prejudices which tend to weaken the spirit of obedience; it is, in fine, a sort of instinct which embraces all those things suggested by zeal and devotion. Can there be anything more agreeable to God, more useful to the Church, or more meritorious, than to foster thus amongst the well-beloved children of God peace, joy, love of vocation, together with union amongst themselves and with their superiors? It is one of the most substantial advantages we have in religion to know that we are never forsaken in life or death; to find always a heart that can compassionate our pains, a hand which sustains us in danger and lifts us when we fall.

Eleventh Characteristic

To have a lively interest in the whole Order, in its works, its success, and its failures

Religious who have the family spirit wish to know everything which concerns the well-being of the different houses. They willingly take their pens to contribute to the edification and satisfy the lawful curiosity of their brethren. They bless God when they hear good news, and grieve at bad news, losses by death, and, above all, scandalous losses of vocation.

Those who would concentrate all their thoughts on their own work, as if all other work counted for nothing or merited no attention, who would speak feebly or perhaps jealously of it, as if they alone wished to do good, or that others wished to deprive them of some glory, would show that they only sought themselves, and that to little love of the Church they joined much indifference for their Order.

Charity, by uniting its good wishes and interest to the deeds of others, becomes associated at the same time in the merit. It shares in a certain manner in the gifts and labours of others. It is, at the same time, the eye, the hand, the tongue, and the foot, since it rejoices at what is done by the eye, the hand, the tongue, etc., or, rather, it is as the soul which presides over all, and to whom nothing is a stranger in the body over which it presides.

Twelfth Characteristic

Mutual Edification

Be edified at the sight of your brethren's virtues, and edify them by your own. In other words, be alternately disciple and master.

Profit by the labours of others, and make them profit by your own. Receive from all, in order to be able to give to all. Borrow humility from one, obedience from another, union with God, and the practice of mortification from others.

By charity we store up in ourselves the gifts of grace enjoyed by every member of the community, in order to dispense them to all by a happy commerce and admirable exchange.

As the bee draws honey from the sweetest juices contained in each flower; as the artist studies the masterpieces to reproduce their marvellous tints in pictures which, in their turn, become models; as a mirror placed in a focus receives the rays of brilliancy from a thousand others placed around it to re-invest them with a dazzling brilliancy, so happy is the community whose members multiply themselves, so to say, by mutually esteeming, loving, admiring, and imitating each other in what is good.

This spontaneity of virtues exercises on all the members a constant and sublime ministry of mutual edification and reciprocal sanctification.

Extent and Delicacy of God's Charity for Men

In order to excite ourselves to fraternal charity, let us try and picture that of God for us. After having had us present in His thoughts from all eternity, He has called us from nothingness to life.

He Himself formed man's body, and, animating it with a breath, enclosed in it an immortal soul, created to His own image. Scarcely arrived on the threshold of life, we found an officer from His court an angel deputed to protect, accompany, and conduct us in triumph to our heavenly inheritance.

What a superb palace He has prepared for us in this world, supplied with a prodigious variety of flowers, fruits, and animals which He has placed at our disposal!

We were a fallen race, and He sent His Son to raise us and save us from hell, which we merited. The Word was made flesh. He took a body and soul like ours, thus ennobling and deifying, so to speak, our human nature. Before ascending to His heavenly Father, after having been immolated for us on the Cross, for fear of leaving us orphans, He wished to remain amongst us in the Holy Eucharist, to nourish us with His flesh, and to infuse into our hearts His Divine Spirit as the living promise and the delicious foretaste of the felicity and glory which He went to prepare for us in His kingdom.

Truly, O God, You treat us not only with a paternal love, but with an infinite respect and honour; and cannot I love and honour those whom You have thus honoured and loved Yourself? Why do not these thoughts inflame my charity in the fire of your Divine love? My brethren and myself are children of God and members of Jesus Christ. My brethren have their angels, who are companions of my angel. One day my brethren will be my companions in glory, chanting eternally the Divine praises. It is but a short time since, with them, I partook of the heavenly banquet of the Most Holy Sacrament, and to-morrow shall do so again.

Extent and Delicacy of the Charity of Jesus Christ During His Mortal Life

Let us now admire the charity of our Divine Saviour while on earth.

If wine was wanting at a feast; if fishermen laboured in vain during the night; if a vast crowd knew not where to procure food in the desert; if unfortunate persons were possessed by devils or deprived of the use of their limbs; if death deprived a father of his daughter, or a widow of an only son, Jesus was there to supply what was wanting, to give back what was lost, or to sweeten all their griefs. Sometimes He forestalled the petition by curing before being asked, or by exciting the wavering faith. He generally went beyond the demands of the petitioners. He was always ready to interrupt His meal, to go to a distance, or to quit His solitude. Nicodemus, as yet trembling and timid, came to find Jesus during the night, and He did not hesitate to sacrifice His sleep by prolonging the conversation. The Samaritan woman was not beneath His notice, although He was fatigued after a long journey. He lavished with prodigality His caresses on the children who pressed around Him. When the crowd was so great that the poor woman with the flow of blood could not come within reach of His hand, He caused an all-powerful virtue to set out from Him, and a simple touch of the hem of His garment supplied instead.

With what charming grace His benefits were accompanied! "Zacheus, come down quickly, for I will abide this day in thy house" (Lk. 19: 5). Who more than He excelled in the art of making agreeable surprises? In His apparitions to Magdalen, to the holy women, to the disciples at Emmaus, did He not pay well for the ointment, the tears, and the perfumes, and the hospitality He received from them? Who is not moved with emotion when he sees his Lord preparing a meal for the Apostles on the lake-shore, or asking Peter thrice to give him an opportunity of publicly repairing his triple denial, "Lovest thou Me?"

Who would not be moved when he hears what St. Clement relates—having heard it from St. Peter—that our Lord was accustomed to watch like a mother with her children near His disciples during their sleep to render them any little service?

O Jesus! the sweetest, the most amiable, the most charitable of the children of men, make me a sharer in Your mildness, Your love, and Your charity.

First Preservative

How to fortify ourselves against uncharitable conversations, the principal danger to fraternal charity

To meditate on what the Holy Scripture says of it: "Place, O Lord, a guard before my mouth" (Ps. 140)—a vigilant sentinel, well armed, to watch, and, if necessary, to arrest in the passing out any unbecoming word —"and a door before my lips," which, being tightly closed, will never let an uncharitable dart escape.

"Shut in your ears with a hedge of thorns," to counteract the tongue, which would pour into them the poison of uncharitableness, "and refuse to listen to the wicked tongue."

"Put before your mouth several doors and on your ears several locks"—i.e., put doors upon doors and locks upon locks, because the tongue is capable, in its fury, to force open the first door and break the first lock. "Melt your gold and silver, and make for your words a balance"—weighing them all before uttering them —"and have for your mouth solid bridles which are tightly held," for fear that the tongue, getting the better of your vigilance, will break loose and do mischief in all directions.

Considering these many barriers and formidable checks, must we not see the necessity of burying in a well-fortified prison that most dangerous monster, the tongue? "Ah! truly death and life are in the power of the tongue" (Prov. 18). "And although the sword has been the instrument of innumerable murders, the tongue has at all times beaten it in producing death" (Ecclus. 28). "It forms but a small part of the body, and has done mighty evil: as the helm badly directed causes the wreck of a fine ship, and as a spark may enkindle a forest. . . . Unquiet evil, inflamed firebrand, source of deadly poison, world of iniquity"(Js. 3: 4).

Second Preservative

To meditate on what the Saints say

St. Bonaventure relates that St. Francis of Assisi said to his religious one day: "Uncharitable conversation is worse than the assassin, because it kills souls and becomes intoxicated with their blood. It is worse than the mad dog, because it tears out and drags on all sides the living entrails of the neighbour. It is worse than the unclean animal, because it wallows in the filth of vices and makes its favourite pasture there. It is worse than Cham, because it exposes everywhere the nasty spots which soil the face of religion—its mother."

St. Bernard goes further: "Do not hesitate to regard the tongue of the backbiter as more cruel than the iron of the lance which pierced our Saviour's side, because it not only pierces His sacred side, but one of His living members also, to whom by its wound it gives death. It is more cruel than the thorns with which His venerable head was crowned and torn, and even than the nails with which the wicked Jews fastened His sacred hands and feet to the Cross, because if our Divine Saviour did not esteem more highly the member of His mystic body (which is pierced by the foul tongue of the slanderer) than His own natural body formed by the operation of the Holy Ghost in the chaste womb of the Virgin Mary, He would never have consented to deliver the latter to ignominies and outrages to spare the former."

Now St. Francis and St. Bernard are here speaking to religious. Is it possible, then, for backbiting to glide into religious communities? Yes, certainly. And it is by this snare that Satan catches souls which have escaped all others.

St. Jerome says: "There are few who avoid this fault. Amongst those even who pride themselves on leading an irreproachable life, you will scarcely find any who do not criticize their brethren."

Rarely, without doubt, but too often, nevertheless, we calumniate at first secretly or with one or two friends, afterwards openly and in public. We speak of the mistakes, shortcomings, and defects, great and small, and sometimes transmit them as a legacy. Sometimes we use a moderate hypocrisy by purposely letting ourselves be questioned, and sometimes brutally attack our victim without shame.

"Have I, then," may the religious thus attacked say, "in making my vows renounced my honour and delivered my character to pillage? Has my position as religious, has the majesty of the King of Kings, of whom I have become the intimate friend, in place of ennobling me, degraded me? You call yourselves my brethren, and yet there are none who esteem me less! You would not steal my money, and yet you make no scruple of stealing my character, a thousand times more precious. You pay court to your Saviour and persecute His child! The same tongue on which reposes the Holy of Holies spreads poison and death! Is this to be the result of your study and practice of virtue? Has not Jesus Christ, by so many Communions, placed a little sweetness on your tongue and a little charity in your heart? By eating the Lamb have you become wolves?," as St. John Chrysostom reproached the clergy of Antioch. "And you, who fly so carefully the gross vices of the world, have you no care or anxiety about damning yourself by slander?"

Third Preservative

To guard the tongue

This must be done especially in five circumstances: (1) At the change of Superiors. Do not criticize the outgoing Superior nor flatter the new one. (2) When you replace another religious. Never by word or act cast any blame on him. Inexperience, or a desire to introduce new customs, sometimes causes this to be done. (3) When you are getting old. Because then we are apt to think—erroneously, of course—that the young members growing up are incapable of fulfilling duties once accomplished by ourselves. (4) When religious come from another house do not ask questions which they ought not to answer, and do not tell them anything which might prejudice or disgust them with the house or anyone in it. Lastly, in our interviews with our particular friends we must be very cautious. There are some who, when anything goes amiss with them, always seek the company of their confidants. These should seriously examine before God whether it is a necessary comfort in affliction or a support in weakness, or the too human satisfaction of justifying themselves, giving vent to their feelings, or getting blame and criticism for the Superior or some one else. They should also examine whether on such occasions they speak the exact truth, and whether they seek a friend, who knows how to take the arrow sweetly from the wound rather than to bury it deeper.

The way to find out the gravity of the sin of detraction is—(1) To consider the position of him who speaks and the weight which is attached to his words; (2) the position of him who is spoken about, and the need he has of his reputation; (3) the evil thing said; (4) the number of the hearers; (5) the result of the detraction; and, lastly, the intention of the speaker, and the passion which was the cause of it.

Fourth Preservative

To be on our guard with certain persons

There are six sorts of religious who wound fraternal charity more or less fatally, (1) Those who say to you, "Such a one said so-and-so about you." These are the sowers of discord, whom God Almighty declares He has in abomination. Their tongues have three fangs more terrible than a viper. "With one blow," says St. Bernard, "they kill three persons—themselves, the listeners, and the absent." (2) Those who, obscuring and perverting this amiable virtue, possess the infernal secret of transforming it into vice. Is not this to sin against the Holy Ghost? (3) Those who skilfully turn the conversation on those brethren of whom they are jealous, in order to have all put in a bad word. They thus double the fault they apparently wish to avoid. (4) Those who constantly have their ears cocked to hear domestic news, who are skilful in finding out secrets and picking up stories, whose trade seems to be to take note of all little bits of scandalous news going, and to take them from ear to ear, or, worse, from house to house. Oh, what an occupation! What a recreation for a spouse of Christ! (5) Those who, under pretext of enlivening the conversation, sacrifice their brethren to the vain and cruel wantonness of witticism by relating something funny in order to give a lash of their tongue or to expose some weakness. Alas! they forget that they ruin themselves in the esteem and opinion of the hearers. (6) Critics of intellectual work. On this point jealousy betrays itself very easily on one side, and susceptibility is stirred on the other. The heart is never insensible nor the mouth silent when we are wounded in so delicate a part. It is evident, besides, that in this case the blame supposes a desire of praise, and that in proportion as we endeavour to lower our brethren we try to raise ourselves. All these religious ought to be regarded as pests in the community.

If we call those who maintain fraternal charity the children of God, should not those who disturb it be called the children of Satan? Do they not endeavour to turn the abode of peace into a den of discord, and the sanctuary of prayer into a porch of hell?

Fifth Preservative

To be cautious in letter-writing and visiting

Great care must be taken never to repeat anything at visits or in letters which might compromise the honour of the community or any of its members.

Never utter a word or write a syllable which might in the least degree diminish the esteem or lower the merit of anyone. Every well-reared person knows that little family secrets must be kept under lock and key.

St. Jane Frances de Chantal writes: "To mention rashly outside the community without great necessity the faults of religious would be great impudence. Never relate outside, even to ecclesiastics, frivolous complaints and lamentations without foundation, which serve only to bring religion, and those who govern therein, into disrepute. Certainly, we ought to be jealous of the honour and good odour of religious houses, which are the family of God. Guard this as an essential point which requires restitution."

Sixth Preservative

Caution in communication with superiors

In communications made to Superiors say the exact truth, and for a good purpose. Do not speak into other ears that which, strictly speaking, should only be told to the local Superior or Superior-General. With the exception of extraordinary cases, or when it refers to a bad habit or something otherwise irremediable, there is generally little charity and less prudence in telling the Superior-General of something blameable which has occurred. Do not reveal, even before a Superior, confidences which conscience, probity, or friendship requires to be guarded with an inviolable seal of friendship. If we write a complaint about a personal offence, lessen it rather than exaggerate, and endeavour to praise the person for good qualities, because nothing is easier than to blacken entirely another's reputation.

Pray and wait till your emotion be calmed. When passion holds the pen, it is no longer the ink that flows, but spleen, and the pen is transformed into a sword.

Before speaking or writing to the Superior it would be well to put this question to ourselves: "Am I one of those proud spirits who expose the faults of others in order to show off their own pretended virtues? or jealous spirits who are offended at the elevation of others? or vindictive spirits who like to give tit for tat? or polite spirits who wish to appear important? or ill-humoured, narrow-minded spirits, scandalized at trifles? or credulous, inconsiderate spirits who believe and repeat everything—the bad rather than the good? In fine, am I a hypocrite who, clothing malice with the mantle of charity, and hiding a cruel pleasure under the veil of compassion, weep with the victim they intend to immolate, as though profoundly touched by his misfortune, and seem to yield only to the imperative demands of duty and zeal?"

Seventh Preservative

Caution in doubtful cases

Act with the greatest reserve in doubtful cases where grave suspicions, difficult to be cleared up, rest on a religious superior or inferior, as the case may be.

The ears of the Superior are sacred, and it is unworthy profanation to pour into them false or exaggerated reports. To infect the Superior's ears is a greater crime than to poison the drinking fountain or to steal a treasure, because the only treasure of religious is the esteem of their Superior, and the pure water which refreshes their souls is the encouraging and benevolent words of the same Superior.

Some, by imprudence or under the influence of a highly coloured or impressionable imagination which carries everything to extremes (we would not say through malice), render themselves often guilty of crying acts of injustice and ruin a religious. What is uncertain they relate as certain, and what is mere conjecture they take as the base of grave suspicions. Several facts which, taken individually, constitute scarcely a fault, they group together, and so make a mountain out of a few grains of sand. An act which, seen in its entirety, would be worthy of praise, they mutilate in such a fashion as to show it in an unfavourable light. Enemies of the positive degree, they lavish with prodigality the words *often, very much, exceedingly,* etc. When they have only one or two witnesses, they make use of the word *everybody,* thereby leaving you under the impression that the rumour is scattered broadcast. On such statements, how can a Superior pronounce judgment?

Eight Preservative

To check uncharitable conversation in others

When you see charity wounded by an equal call him to order.

If to say or do anything scandalous is the first sin forbidden by charity, not to stop, when you can, him who speaks or acts badly ought to be considered the second.

When the discourse degenerates, represent Jesus Christ entering suddenly into the midst of the company, and saying, as He did formerly to the disciples of Emmaus: "What discourse hold you among yourselves, and why are you sad?" (Lk. 24: 17) Recall also these words of the Psalmist: "You have preferred to say evil rather than good, and to relate vices rather than virtues. O deceitful, inconsiderate, and rash tongue! Dost thou think thou wilt remain unpunished? No; God will punish thee in everlasting flames" (Ps. 51: 5-8) After having thus fortified ourselves against uncharitable conversation, we ought to try and put a stop to it.

St. John Climacus tells us to address the following words to those who calumniate in our presence: "For mercy's sake cease such conversation! How would you wish me to stone my brethren—me, whose faults are greater and more numerous?"

A holy religious replied to an uncharitable person: "We have to render infinite thanks to God if we are not such as those of whom you speak. Alas! what would become of us without Him?"

The philosopher Zeno, hearing a man relate a number of misdeeds about Antisthenes, said to him: "Ah! Has he never done anything good? Has he never done anything for which he merits praise?" "I don't know," he replied. Then said Zeno, "How is that? You have sufficient perception to remark, and sufficient memory to remember, this long list of faults, and you have had no eyes to see his many good qualities and virtuous actions."

St. John Chrysostom says: "To the calumniator I wish you to say the following: If you can praise your neighbours, my ears are open to receive your perfume. If you can only blacken them, my ears are closed, as I do not wish them to be the receptacle of your filthy words. What matters it to me to hear that such a one is wicked, and has done some detestable act? Friend, think of the account that must be rendered to the Sovereign Judge.

What excuse can we give, and what mercy will we deserve—we who have been so keen-sighted to the faults of others, and so blind to our own? You would consider it very rude for a person to look into your private room; but I say it is far worse to pry into another's private life and to expose it."

The calumniator should remember that, besides the fault he commits and the wrong he does to his neighbours, he exposes himself, by a just punishment of God, to be the victim of calumny himself.

Ninth Preservative

How to check uncharitable conversation in superiors, etc.

When we see charity wounded by persons worthy of respect, keep silent, in order to show your regret, or relate something to the advantage of the absent. If necessary, withdraw.

It is related in the life of Sister Margaret, of the Blessed Sacrament of the Carmelite Order, that when a discourse against charity took place in the house she saw a smoke arise of such suffocating odour that she nearly fainted, and fled immediately to her Divine Master for pardon.

St. Jerome, writing to Nepotian on this subject, says: "Some object that they cannot warn the speaker of his fault without failing in the respect due to him. This excuse is vain, because their eagerness to listen increases his itch for speaking. No one wishes to relate calumnies and murmurs to ears closed with disgust. Is there anyone so foolish as to shoot arrows against a stone wall?" Let your strict silence be a significant and salutary lesson for the detractor. "Have no commerce with those who bite," said Solomon, because perdition is on the eve of overtaking them; and who can tell the disaster and ruin with which the rash detractor and equally blamable listener are threatened?

If it be true, according to the testimony of a religious who was visitor of the houses of his Order, that the virtue against which one can most easily commit a grievous sin in religion is charity; and, according to St. Francis de Sales, sins of the tongue number three-fourths of all sins committed; cannot it be said with equal truth that to refuse to listen to detractors is with one blow to prevent the sin and safeguard charity?

In many cases one can adroitly make known the good qualities and virtues which more than counterbalance the defects related by the defamer. To act thus is to spread about the good odour of Christ.

Tenth Preservative

Be cautious after hearing uncharitable conversation

After having heard uncharitable words, observe the following precautions given by the Saints:

1. Repeat nothing.

2. Believe all the good you hear, but believe only the bad you see. Malice does the contrary. It demands proofs for good reports, but believes bad reports on the slightest grounds. Out of every thousand reports one can scarcely be found accurate in all its details. When, as a rule of prudence, Superiors are told to believe only half of what they hear, to consider the other half, and still suspect the remaining part, what rule should be prescribed for inferiors?

When the act is evidently blameworthy, suppose a good intention, or at least one not so bad as apparent, leaving to God what He reserves to Himself the judgment of the heart; or consider it as the result of surprise, inadvertence, human frailty, or the violence of the temptation. Never come to hasty conclusions—e.g., "He is incorrigible; as he is, so will he always be." Expect everything from grace, efforts, and time.

3. Efface as much as possible the bad impression produced on the mind, because calumny always produces such.

The recital of something bad about a fellow-religious based on probabilities has sufficed to tarnish a reputation which ample apologies cannot fully repair. The detractor's evil reports are believed on account of the audacity with which he relates them, but when he wants to relate something good he will not be believed on oath. We know by experience that evil reports spread with compound interest, while good ones are retailed at discount.

Eleventh Preservative

Not to judge or suspect rashly

Expel every doubt, every thought, likely to diminish esteem. They amuse themselves with a most dangerous game who always gather up vague thoughts of the past, rumours without foundation, conjectures in which passion has the greatest share, and thus form in their minds characters of their brethren—adding always, never subtracting—and by dint of the high idea they have of their own ability conclude that all their judgments are true, and thus become fixed in their bad habit. St. Bernard, comparing them to painters, warns them that it is the devil who furnishes the materials, and even the evil conceptions, necessary to depict such bad impressions of their brethren. We read in the *Life of St. Francis* that our Lord Himself called in a distinct voice a certain young man to his Order. "O Lord," replied the young man, "when I am once entered, what must I do to please You?" Pay particular attention to our Lord's answer: "Lead thou a life in common with the rest. Avoid particular friendships. Take no notice of the defects of others, and form no unfavourable judgments about them." What matter for consideration in these admirable words!

Thomas à Kempis says: "Turn thy eyes back upon thyself, and see thou judge not the doing of others. In judging others a man labours in vain, often errs, and easily sins; but in judging and looking into himself he always labours with fruit. We frequently judge of a thing according to the inclination of our hearts, because self-love easily alters in us a true judgment."

Rodriguez tells us to turn on ourselves the sinister questions, etc., we are tempted to refer to others e.g.: "It is I who am deceived. It is through jealousy that I condemn my brethren. It is through malice that I find so much to blame in them. Finally, the fault is mine, not theirs."

Even when reports more or less true might depreciate in your eyes some of the community, may they not have, besides their faults, some great but hidden virtues, and by these be entitled to a more merciful judgment? St. Augustine says beautifully: "If you cast your eye over a field where the corn has been trampled, you only perceive the straw, not the grain. Lift up the straw, and you will see plenty of golden sheaves full of grain." The simile is very applicable to a poor religious beaten down by foul tongues. We blame the defects of our brethren, and perhaps we have the same, or others more shameful still. We usurp the right of judgment, which God reserves to Himself, and forget that He will punish us by leaving us to our own irregular passions. Ah! is it not already a very great misfortune to have these contemptuous, slanderous, distrustful thoughts, and many other sins, the result of malicious suspicions and rash judgments, rooted in the soul?

Means to Support the Evil Thoughts and Tongues of Others

What must be done in those painful moments when, being the victim of a painful calumny, the object of suspicion, the butt of domestic persecution, we are tempted to believe that charity is banished from the community, and so to banish it from our own heart? Recall the words of St. John of the Cross. "Imagine," says he, "that your brethren are so many sculptors armed with mallets and chisels, and that you have been placed before them as a block of marble destined in the mind of God to become a statue representing the Man of Sorrows, Jesus crucified." Consider a hasty word said to you as a thorn in the head; a mockery as a spit in the face; an unkind act as a nail in the hand; a hatred which takes the place of friendship as a lance in the side; all that which hurts, contradicts, or humiliates us as the blows, stripes, the gall and vinegar, the crown of thorns and the cross. The work proceeds always, sometimes slowly, sometimes quickly. Let us not complain. We will one day thank these workmen, who, without intending it, give to our soul the most beautiful, the most glorious, and the noblest traits. We ourselves are sculptors as well as statues, and we will find that, on our part, we have materially helped to form in them the same traits.

"If all were perfect," says the *Imitation*, "what, then, should we have to suffer from others for God's sake?"

It is not forbidden us to seek consolation. But from whom? Is it from those discontented spirits whose ears are like public sewers, the receptacle of every filth and dirt? They increase our pain by pouring the poison of their own discontent instead of the oil of the Good Samaritan. They will take our disease and give us theirs, and, like Samson's foxes, spread destruction around by repeating what we said to them. May God preserve us from this misfortune! If we cannot carry our burden alone, and if we find it no relief to lay our griefs in the Sacred Heart of Jesus, let us go to him whom the rule appoints to be our friend and consoler, our confidant and director, and who, as St. Augustine relates of St. Monica, after having listened to us with patience, charity, and compassion, after having at first appeared to share our sentiments, will sweeten and explain all with prudence, will lift up and encourage our oppressed heart, and by his counsel and prayers will restore us to peace and charity.

Second Means to Bear with Others

Recall the words of our Lord to Blessed Margaret Mary: "With the intention of perfecting thee by patience I will increase thy sensibility and repugnance, so that thou wilt find occasions of humiliation and suffering even in the smallest and most indifferent things."

What would be considered, when we were in the world, as the prick of a needle, we look upon in religion as the blow of a sword. What we looked upon in our own house as light as a feather, becomes in community life as heavy as a rock. An insignificant word becomes an outrage, and a little matter which formerly would escape our notice now upsets us, and even deprives us of sleep and appetite. Is not this increase of sensibility and repugnance found in the religious state only to form in us the image of our crucified Lord? If Christ alone has suffered interiorly more than all the Saints and Martyrs together, was it not because of this extreme repugnance of His soul, which multiplied to infinity for Him the bitterness of the affronts and the rigour of His torments? Religious may expect for a certainty that, like their Divine Master, there are reserved for them moments of complete abandonment, those agonies intended for the souls of the elect, in which Nature seems on the point of succumbing. No consolation from their families, which they have quitted; nor from their companions, who are busy in their various employments; nor from their Superiors, who do not understand the excess of their grief, and whose words by Divine permission produce no effect.

The solemn moment of agony with our Divine Saviour was that in which, abandoned, betrayed, and denied by His Apostles, and perceiving in His Father only an irritated face, He exclaimed, "My God! My God! why hast Thou forsaken Me?" Such will be for religious the last touch which will complete in them the resemblance of Jesus crucified, provided they will render themselves worthy of it.

When will be the time of this complete abandonment? How long will this agony be prolonged? This is a secret known only to God.

Conclusion

Poverty, chastity, obedience, and charity—such are the virtues suitable and characteristic of the religious. In this little treatise we have endeavoured to trace the features of the last.

In every community we can distinguish two sorts of religious— those who mount and those who descend— those whose face is towards the path of perfection, and those who have turned their back to it. Perhaps amongst these latter some have only one more step to abandon it altogether. Now we mount or descend, proceed or retrace our steps, in proportion as we practise these four virtues or neglect them.

Fraternal Charity

A religious Order is like a fire balloon, which requires four conditions in order to rise into the clouds amidst the applause of the spectators. First, the rarefaction of the air by fire. This represents the vow of poverty, which empties the heart through the hands, and substitutes the desire of heavenly goods for those of earth. Second, release from the cords which bind it down. This represents the effects of the vow of chastity, which, by breaking human attachments, permits us to soar towards God with freedom and rapidity. Third, a man who will feed the fire and moderate the flight of the balloon upwards. This represents the right which the vow of obedience places in the hands of the Superior, to nourish the sacred fire, and direct the sublime movement of the soul and foresee dangers. Fourth, the union of its component parts. This represents the operations of charity, in causing all the members of a community to have but one heart and one soul.

Possessing these four virtues, a religious Order soars in the heights of perfection; but if one of these be wanting it falls helplessly, and is no longer an object of edification, but of scandal and ridicule.

When it happens that some members, losing the spirit of their state, abandon their holy vocation, we may say with St. John: "They went out from us; but they were not of us. For if they had been of us, they would no doubt have continued with us: but that they might be made manifest that they are not all of us" (1 Jn. 2: 19).

They appeared to have the religious virtues, but in reality one or all were wanting to them.

O God, do not permit that lukewarmness or an uncontrolled passion will ever make me waver in my vocation. During life and at death I wish to remain a faithful religious, so that I may find the salvation which Thou hast promised by procuring Thy glory. As good grain improves by pulling up the weeds, and the body becomes healthy when purged of bad humours, pour into my soul the grace and unction which others refuse, in order that, practising more perfectly from day to day poverty, chastity, obedience, and charity, and redoubling my ardour and zeal to my last hour, I may obtain the priceless treasure promised to those who have quitted all to follow Thee. Amen.

Appendix

The Practice of Fraternal Charity (Fr. Faber)

1. Often reflect on some good point in each of your brethren.

2. Do this most in the case of those whom we are most inclined to criticize.

3. Never claim rights or even let ourselves feel that we have them, as this spirit is most fatal both to obedience and charity.

4. Charitable thoughts are the only security of charitable deeds.

5. Never have an aversion for another, much less manifest itself.

6. Avoid particular friendships.

7. Never judge another. Always, if possible, excuse the faults we see, and if we cannot excuse the action, excuse the intention. We cannot all think alike, and we should, therefore, avoid attributing bad motives to others.

Charitable Religious

They have a disregard of self and a desire to accommodate others. They rejoice with their companions in their joys and recreations, and grieve with them in their afflictions.

They try to bring all the good they can to the community and to avert all the evil. They begin with themselves, by being as little trouble as possible to others.

With great charity and affability they bear with the faults and shortcomings of others, careful to fulfil the law of Christ, which tells us to bear one another's burdens.

They dispense to others what they have for their own advantage; more particularly do they give spiritual assistance by prayer and the other spiritual works of mercy.

They never contradict anyone. They never speak against anyone. They are convinced that charity, holy friendships, and concord form the great solace of this life, and that no good ever came from dissensions and disputes.

They consider that God is ever in the midst of those who live united together by the bonds of holy love.

We will do likewise if we consider the image of God in the souls of our brethren. As we form one body here and one spirit in the same faith and charity, let us hope not to be separated hereafter, but to belong for ever to that one body in heaven when faith and hope shall disappear, but where charity alone shall remain, and remain for ever.

www.ingramcontent.com/pod-product-compliance
Lightning Source LLC
Chambersburg PA
CBHW050045080526
44586CB00014B/1465